"If you believe workforce development is a social justice issue, this is a relevant guide to propel the reader into accelerated personal & professional growth. Each story will help you navigate and learn lessons that others have successfully navigated with black and brown bruises along the way. It's a must-read for the career conscious! This book compels us to take the next step toward success!"

Jennifer C. Joyner
University Relations
Workforce Development Strategist

"Rebecca Taylor encapsulates Black Americans' obstacles in reaching professional aspirations but takes it one level higher in examining authenticity to self. Many of us have clear paths on what professional success means, shaped by our community and others, with very little guidance on personal success and how we internally measure achievement. I recommend this book for any Black American and their allies on how to best outline their path to success for true personal and professional joy."

Kamila Elliott, CFP®
CEO of Collective Wealth Partners
First black Chair of the CFP Board

"In Stay or Go: Five Breakthrough Steps for Career Transitions™ - The Black Professional Narrative, Rebecca Taylor offers a compelling and insightful resource for Black professionals at a career crossroads. By blending personal narratives, strategic guidance, and practical steps, Taylor creates a roadmap that empowers readers to navigate their professional journeys with clarity and purpose. This book is a valuable companion for anyone seeking to transcend workplace challenges and pursue fulfilling career transitions while staying true to their authentic selves."

Reggie Richardson
Financial Services
International Executive

stay or go

Five Breakthrough
Steps for Career Transitions™

The Black Professional Narrative

Rebecca Taylor

JT Publishing House

Requests to the author for permission should be addressed to:
JT Publishing House, writing@jtpublishinghouse.com

Names: Taylor, Rebecca.
Title: Stay/ Rebecca Taylor.
Description: Spartanburg: JT Publishing House, 2023. | Summary: "The
Five Breakthrough Steps for Career Transitions is a roadmap for anyone
contemplating which career direction is next for them. It's written as a guide
to navigating the moments when you stop and question your professional
journey—whether you should stay on your current career path or with
your current employer. It's written to support your desire to pursue a new
position, new company, new industry, or any career transition that shifts you
and your responsibilities. "-- Provided by publisher.

Identifiers: LCCN 2023944762 (print) | ISBN 9781954624979 (paperback) |
ISBN 9781954624962 (ebook)
Subjects: BISAC: Business & Economics /Careers/ General

LC record available at https://lccn.loc.gov/2023944762

Disclaimer: Any internet addresses (websites, blogs, etc.) and telephone
numbers in this book are offered as a resource. They are not intended in any
way to be or imply an endorsement by JT Publishing House or the author,
nor does JT Publishing House vouch for the content of these sites and
numbers for the life of this book.

Published by JT Publishing, Spartanburg, South Carolina
www.jtpublishinghouse.com

Printed in the United States of America
10 9 8 7 6 5 4 3 2 1

STAY OR GO

Five Breakthrough
Steps for Career Transitions™

The Black Professional Narrative

Rebecca Taylor

CONTENTS

INTRODUCTION

In 2020, the world was on fire following the killing of George Floyd in Minneapolis, Minnesota. This occurrence was yet another moment in a five-year span when a police officer killed a Black man. I was beyond tired and triggered, to the point that I contemplated joining local protests.

I found myself at the intersection of social distancing due to the COVID-19 pandemic and social unrest. I was no longer willing or able to code-switch or compartmentalize societal impacts at work, even while connecting virtually.

The fatigue of making others comfortable with my presence was and is a heavy burden. My presence as a Black, highly ambitious, talented millennial woman transitioning from middle to senior management in Corporate America brought on new weights and responsibilities. I was discerning how I wanted my voice to be heard and felt.

Was it through protesting?

Was it through social media?

Between reading articles and news alerts and scrolling endlessly through a spectrum of polarized comments, I quickly realized posting would not help me cope. And frankly, in dealing with the traumatic triggers, I felt like I was allowed and justified to be silent, so I prioritized protecting my peace.

My resolve was to have an impact in a different way. I became an outlet for my friends, family, and professional network. I cultivated a circle of support to hold conversations to unpack the trauma and affirm each other by placing self-care over educating anyone who couldn't believe what was happening or how we got "here."

My catharsis was facilitating Diversity, Equity, and Inclusion (DEI) discussions on social issues for all ethnic groups at work.

We spent time learning, reflecting, and determining how to support each other. That ongoing dialogue opened the door to coaching conversations revealing that many of my colleagues, particularly Black professionals, were considering career transitions.

They were ready to transition because, on the other side of their fatigue, they wanted to occupy work environments where they were seen, heard, and valued. The reality of what each person was carrying and their adjustments to navigate their career ignited a desire to make a change.

Transition to what?

Transition how?

Transition when?

We work hard to prove our value and worth to ourselves, our peers, our leaders, and our organization while masking family divorce, financial responsibility, sickness, caring for loved ones, and being afraid for the lives of our family and friends. We show up at work, turning parts of us and our lives off because we're constantly working to make people comfortable with our presence.

While we carry this pressure, life moments can shine a light of reflection that "this work environment may not be for me."

The intersection of the pandemic and social injustices ignited the realization that we are tired. We hold the power to choose if we stay or go.

You may be standing at a crossroads determining if you should stay or go, perhaps for different reasons. Regardless of your reasons, this book is your roadmap if you're contemplating which career direction is next.

It's written as a guide to help navigate the moments when you stop and question your professional journey—whether you should stay on your current career path with your current employer or go and explore new options. It's intended to support your desire to pursue a new position, company, industry, or any career transition that shifts you and your responsibilities. Whether it's a new professional endeavor or entrepreneurship, this book will equip you with the steps to discern how to move forward so you're prepared to navigate any career transition.

This book is purposefully geared to support Black professionals seeking a career transition by highlighting the Black experience, and it intends to concretize the notion that Black stories are human stories. While the Black experience transcends cultures and there are commonalities our non-Black counterparts can acknowledge, I wanted to help other Black professionals wrestling with career decisions by sharing experiences from people who look like us.

WHY BLACK PROFESSIONALS?

It became clear that the career challenges, the internal talk, and the coaching conversations within my network were far-reaching dialogues that required more attention, support, and resources.

Personally, I understand the impact of aggression, the fatigue of making people comfortable with your presence, and the doubt and fear of pivoting away from something known. I also understand the risk and concerns if a career transition doesn't work out, the desire for tools to navigate your career successfully, and the self-limiting beliefs that hold us back—real or imagined.

During my career transitions, I carefully considered what steps I took in the seasons when I questioned if I should stay or whether it was time to go.

The Five Breakthrough Steps for Career Transitions™ I developed helped me and professionals I coached get to the other side of that decision.

THE FIVE BREAKTHROUGH STEPS FOR CAREER TRANSITIONS™

Step 1: Assess Where You Are

Step 2: Determine What You Want

Step 3: Strategize Your Next Best Move

Step 4: Take a Step

Step 5: Reflect and Redirect

While these five steps are not linear, I recommend exploring each area to clarify your decision-making. To help you learn how to apply each step practically, I interviewed 12 Black professionals–five men and seven women with various backgrounds, marital statuses, and unique career transition experiences across six industries in Corporate

America, from middle to senior-level roles.

I trust pieces of their background and stories will resonate with you. Through their stories, you'll learn more about my Five Breakthrough Steps for Career Transitions™, how they were applied, and how they helped each person navigate their career transitions. Through their experiences, you will have the opportunity to reflect and consider how to use each step to guide your transition.

PART I

MY CAREER TRANSITION STORY

I come from a lineage of teachers—my grandparents, parents, aunts, uncles, cousins, and godparents. My mother is the seventh child of ten siblings. Six of my maternal aunts and uncles were teachers, vice principals, principals, or educators in some capacity.

My parents are part of a generation of Black Southerners from the United States who migrated North upon graduating from Historically Black Colleges and Universities in the late 1960s and early 1970s for better work opportunities. They picked a career and an employer and stuck with it until retirement because they based career decisions on stability.

Early on, my mother wanted to become a flight attendant. At my grandmother's advice, she opted to choose teaching as a more "stable" career. My mother proudly boasts she taught for 38 years. Upon retirement, she had no desire to keep working in any form.

My father, on the other hand, retired, then continued to work for several years until his health no longer allowed him. Retirement without any work responsibilities was an adjustment for him. At various points in his life, my father worked three jobs to provide for our family and extend kindness and generosity to others.

Naturally, I considered becoming a teacher (despite having the nickname lawyer as a child from a family friend because of the number of questions I asked). During a visit to my mother's classroom on "take your child to work day," I realized her classroom of students required a different level of patience than I, at eight years old, could see myself embodying.

Then there was a period when I thought I'd become a clothing designer or a hairstylist. I have sketch pads and hair crimpers as reminders of less-traveled career paths. I was quite a young entrepreneur as well. My early endeavors included a book club, a hair wrap business, jewelry making, babysitting, and cleaning services. I played tennis, soccer, volleyball, basketball, and ran track. I participated in writing camps, archeology (yes, I dug in the dirt looking for fossils in the middle of summer), and drama classes.

I even completed week-long pre-college business and arts and humanities programs at the University of Wisconsin Whitewater. I had exposure to all these programs and activities before high school. I appreciate that my parents ensured I had access to different programs, enrichment classes, camps, and sports. Throughout all of it, I don't recall them advising me on how to decide on a career or guiding me to a particular path.

The learning opportunities and range of experiences my parents immersed me in established a foundation to explore my own path. I held leadership roles in high school on the student council and sports teams. I also took an elective leadership and ethics course and became somewhat drawn to psychology.

Somewhere along the way, I narrowed in on business because I believed that path would provide a better salary. My business focus allowed me to be intentional in my college search. I passed on any college that wouldn't accept me as a freshman directly into their business school.

Although I was still deciding what area of business to major in initially, I knew finance and accounting were too numbers based for me. Still intrigued by psychology, I considered a minor but wasn't interested in being in school "forever" to put psychology to use.

Life experiences, a college professor, and ideas about professions that provide a better salary led me to major in Human Resources (HR) with a minor in Information Systems. Once I declared my studies, my godmother recommended I apply to INROADS– an organization that develops and places talented minority youth in business and industry.

I didn't know much about navigating the business world and didn't have representation around me. Still, I quickly learned I needed internships to help me narrow down my newly declared major and minor if I wanted to find a job after graduation. Through two INROADS internships at a financial services company based in Milwaukee, Wisconsin, I gained exposure to HR Training/Development and Recruiting with broader opportunities to learn about Corporate HR areas and the industry.

Saturday INROADS training sessions taught me how to navigate Corporate America. I didn't realize then that this would be the beginning of navigating career transitions for me. I had clarity in my aspirations to pursue a career in HR within Recruiting in the financial services and investment industry at the most inopportune time —2008-2009. As I prepared to graduate and start this exciting, well-paid HR recruiting job in financial services, the world entered an economic recession following the US mortgage crisis.

After graduation, I humbly returned home without a job. Thankfully, I maintained working two jobs—my retail department store job and summer internships during the last two years of college. I took on full-time retail hours and interviewed for as many available HR opportunities as possible. When that plan didn't yield results, I strategized my next best move—transition to another retail job that would pay more and provide HR hiring responsibilities.

The following year I gained more

HR and leadership responsibilities while strengthening my desire for a full-time HR role. I eventually landed a position at an HR Shared Services company supporting employment verifications and background checks. While in the role, I began strategizing again. This time, I planned on moving to Charlotte, North Carolina.

At the time, Charlotte ranked number two for banking. I rationalized that despite the 9-10% unemployment rate, I would find a job in Charlotte while still living in Milwaukee. If not, plan B was to return to school full-time and pursue my MBA. I worked, interviewed, and studied for the GMAT. Then life happened in the most beautiful way—the company laid me off. The recession impacted the hiring volume of the biggest client I supported. I took it as a sign to pivot. I remember being happy that I could activate my plan to move to Charlotte.

Thankfully, plans for how I could transition to Charlotte were already in motion. The company let me go on Friday, February 18, 2011, and I didn't miss a beat in strategizing my next best move.

I had the support of my mother and wisely delayed telling my father about the move until about two to three weeks prior to leaving. I knew my father would have concerns and attempt to talk me out of moving, so I shared the news once I settled all the details.

His reaction was as expected, "Rebecca, how will you find a job with so many people out of work? We don't know anyone down there. How will we get to you if something happens?"

My mother reasoned, "You can always come back home if it doesn't work out."

To this day, that reasoning has been the most enduring comfort to sustain me. When I have questioned various career moves, I am assured that I can always go home if it doesn't work out. Knowing I had options and coming to terms with the least ideal scenario freed me of the fear of making a move —to take a step. Six weeks later, on April 1, 2011, I moved to Charlotte without a job.

On April 12, 2011, I started a temporary assignment supporting an HR Information Systems team at the world's largest contract food service company. A few weeks into my work assignment, I saw an unnamed job posting for a contract HR Employment

Coordinator role for a large financial services company on an employment agency's website.

Although another "temporary" job, this one was a contract assignment that had the prospect of becoming a permanent full-time role. Five months into the contract assignment, I secured a full-time position. I landed the ideal HR entry point role at a renowned investment company. Albeit, two years after graduating, things lined up. Since then, I've had the opportunity to transition to eight different roles within the company across three HR subdivisions— Talent Acquisition, HR Business Partners/ Consultant, and Talent Development.

After six years working in Charlotte, I transitioned into a leadership role, completed my Master of Business Administration (MBA), and earned an Executive Coaching certificate. I then decided to gain exposure to more career opportunities which led me to relocate from North Carolina to Pennsylvania for a role in the corporate office. Navigating a new city that wasn't nearly as transient as Charlotte, along with being in a position that wasn't manifesting into the career opportunity I thought it would, left me questioning my decision to prioritize my career and expand my access to opportunities through this move.

In that season, I assessed where I was and revisited what I wanted. I want to excel to an executive role in HR within the organization, so I reframed my mindset and focused on my options. I ultimately realized just that—I had options. I was the one who chose to move to advance my career to better position myself to build a legacy.

I could leave when I no longer wanted to follow that path or felt the city or company wasn't serving me well—even if I didn't have a job lined up. I had done it before; I could do it again. I considered what support I would need if I left without a new opportunity.

How would I cover my expenses?

I could rent my house to cover the mortgage payment and eliminate all the utility bills. I could opt for forbearance on my student loans. I didn't have a car payment and could find ways to reduce other expenses. Or, I could sell my house and utilize the gains to sustain and cover any costs. I could take a mini-sabbatical. I could find a new job. I could launch a coaching practice. I could consult.

Where would I live?

I could stay in Pennsylvania, nestle into a friend's basement apartment, and become her live-in nanny with the bonus of family meals and vacations. Or, I could take that open invite from Ma and move back home to Milwaukee to regroup.

I figured out my worst-case, less-than-ideal, and most humbling scenario. Doing so freed me from thinking I had to stay in a role where I wasn't happy or that didn't align with my passions.

Knowing my least ideal scenario allowed me to strategize my next best move and take a step. Once I had my options, I decided my next best move was to stay in Pennsylvania, pursue a job change, continue fostering relationships with my small network of transient friends, and spend time traveling.

Reflecting on my career transitions, I can now conceptualize the framework—The Five Breakthrough Steps for Career Transitions™ with an overlay of The Black Professional Narrative to provide a practical guide to help you navigate your career transitions.

WHAT'S KEEPING YOU?

Several factors keep us in a role, career path, and organization. It could be a passion for the work, expertise, and skill set, ability to continue to excel, job stability, company familiarity, that next bonus, company investment, loyalty, working relationships, personal and life responsibilities, complacency, fear, anxiety, uncertainty, being overwhelmed, or feeling stuck without knowing how to move forward.

Black professionals especially wrestle with doubt.

I doubt another organization will be any better.

I doubt I will fit in or be accepted in

that company's culture.

I doubt I can transition to a new area of interest or role.

I doubt my experiences qualify me for that higher-level position.

I doubt, given my personal responsibilities, I can successfully navigate the transition to a new opportunity.

I doubt I can maintain the same level of work-life integration.

I doubt I have a strong enough network.

Imposter syndrome is real for many in Corporate America—from women to first-generation college students and career switchers. It especially hits differently for minorities—particularly Black professionals who are navigating cultural norms in a working environment predominantly established by the white majority.

A lot of career doubt for Black professionals is compounded by limited corporate exposure and representation. Various studies highlight the disparate impact imposter syndrome has on minorities. The self-doubt of whether we belong and if our skills, experiences, and pedigree are enough can add up and cause many to forgo pursuing other opportunities for fear of being found a fraud.

Also, the microaggressions Black professionals experience are exhausting and contribute to heightened feelings of imposter syndrome. Things like:

"Your confidence is so interesting to me."

"You're so articulate."

"You have a way with words."

"He's definitely a salesman, but I'm not sure if he has what it takes."

"She's so polished, almost too polished."

"I can tell her involvement in (insert minority professional development organization) helped prepare her to ace the interview."

"I question their authenticity."

"They lack professional [or] executive presence, and their leadership impact could be better."

"That was a flippant comment."

I could go on and on, listing the various microaggressions directed at me, my peers, my direct reports, my friends, and my family at some point.

I've said, "You can't make this stuff up," often enough that it may become the working title for my next book. It would highlight how I've learned to advocate for myself and others, mitigate bias, and not allow others to project their stuff—their insecurities and feelings based on predispositions and ideas held up as the only way or the standard.

The reality is—while I, my village, and my circle of Black professionals walk confidently day in and day out—it's to affirm for ourselves and others that we belong. We have often not been afforded the same grace as others to show up unprepared, unpolished, inarticulate, tentative with a translucent door to our lives, AND still be taken seriously.

Black professionals look around and see limited representation the higher they excel while diligently seeking ways to brand themselves as strategic thought partners. It has impacted the confidence and psychological safety of some, leaving them with more questions than answers. To cope, some have chosen to alter their style to become more palpable, some choose to fall back or recalibrate their ambitions, and others decide to exit stage left.

If you're nodding along in acknowledgment that one, some, or all of these factors are keeping you, it's time to determine if YOU will stay or go.

PART II

THE FIVE BREAKTHROUGH STEPS FOR CAREER TRANSITIONS

STEP 1

ASSESS WHERE YOU ARE

MEET AUTUMN EQUINOX
Age: 33
Industry: Financial Services
Marital status: Single, no children

"It's just a Tax ID; it doesn't have a heartbeat," Autumn Equinox said as she thought about her company and how often she had considered whether to stay or go.

Autumn is a financial service professional with a decade of experience. More importantly, she identifies as a daughter, a caretaker, and a Black woman who aspires to live a legacy of empowering other Black women to see potential in themselves far greater than the world may tell them.

Every year, Autumn reflects on how her development and the company's investment align with her aspirations. Autumn has seen far too many examples of corporations missing the mark on investing in their employees' development in meaningful ways that help them excel and level up in their careers.

As she approaches ten years with her organization, she continues to grow and reap her company's investment. Autumn has participated in various company-led development programs, received company sponsorship for an executive Master of Business Administration (MBA) degree, and gained advocacy for her career aspirations through strategic roles and enterprise initiatives.

Autumn's tenacity to remain reflective about her growth has led her to strategic roles that have aided her development. Being keenly aware of cultural nuances in her organization, she quickly assessed her need to transition to a new role four months into taking a new position. Before joining the team, Autumn was diligent in assessing the role. She understood the essential skills and insight needed to make an impact. Through her network, Autumn gained insight into the environment and team dynamics of the group. Although the group had some opportunities related to inclusion, she was ready to help improve the culture.

Autumn was thoughtful during her onboarding, observing first, then seeking ways to support inclusion throughout the division. After a couple of months, the environment wore on her well-being. When Autumn logged off in the evening, she was fatigued by a day filled with navigating a team environment that commanded a singular style. It was rocking the core of her engagement and belonging.

Amidst heightened social injustices in the United States, she had little desire or energy to engage with family and friends. At night Autumn found herself in perseverance mode, conserving her energy to combat the daunting feeling of starting another day. Before Autumn decided if she would stay or go, she started to assess what was happening and the contributing factors to her experience by reflecting on various scenarios and encounters with the team.

If you're reading this book, you likely want to transition to a new role within your organization or a new company, to a new industry, or to pursue a new career endeavor. Your company culture may be impacting your interest in making a transition. Or perhaps your work is misaligned with your skillset or passion. You may be growing and evolving in ways your current environment doesn't foster, or the environment no longer serves you well. Maybe your lifestyle or family needs are prompting your desire for change. Before jumping to what you could do next, reflect on your current state. It will help you identify areas that are less than ideal and where there are bright spots. This level of mindfulness will allow you to consider what's most important to you and areas you may need to develop.

The ability to assess where you are is a critical first step before considering a career transition. The assessment requires a level of humility and self-introspection. Reflect upon several key career dimensions to gain the necessary clarity to help you determine what you want. Each career-related statement below will help you discern different aspects of where you are. Included are Autumn's reflections on each career dimension.

1. **Is my current work engaging and meaningful?**

Autumn found the work in her new position less engaging than in her prior role. She began questioning the need for her role and saw opportunities to restructure the team to better support the broader division.

2. **Is my performance yielding strong outcomes and impact on the organization?**

Review notes from your one-on-one conversations with your leader and past performance reviews to ensure you're objectively assessing your performance. This assessment will help uncover the value you bring to the organization and opportunities to improve your performance.

In your review, further consider the following:

- What contributions are you bringing to your role, team, and organization?

- What indicators or feedback have you received on your value to the organization?
- Where are there opportunities for you to improve your performance?

- In what areas are you aligned or mis-aligned with your leader (or team) on your outcomes and impact?

- What is contributing to your strong results and impact?

- What is preventing you from delivering solid outcomes and impact?

Autumn had great feedback from key business partners and delivered impactful and meaningful outcomes through company initiatives.

Her unassailable track record of success had led others to recommend her to lead a team that needed a strong leader who would foster an inclusive environment.

She had a proven ability to develop high-potential talent. However, Autumn observed a need for more openness to cultivate different leadership styles. She reflected on her ability to deliver strong outcomes in the current environment fostered by the leadership team.

3. Are my talents and passions aligned?

Reflect on where your talents, areas of passion, or interests exist. The alignment of your abilities and interests is essential to driving your engagement and certainly influences your performance.

You may have innate skills and talents, yet they aren't aligned with your true passion. Uncovering where there is alignment (or misalignment) will provide you with insight to consider if there's potential upskilling or more introspection you need to discover your true passions.

Autumn was skilled in developing talent and analyzing data trends to prioritize strategic initiatives that effectively delivered business value. However, her new department's singular working style approach did not foster her passion for helping others excel and see their potential.

4. **Do I have strong relationships that include mentors, advocates, and sponsors in my network?**

Understanding the network capital you have (or don't) will help you determine who you can connect with to help you reflect, talk through your career options, and advocate for you. Thinking about the internal and external relationships you have developed throughout your career is essential. Consider what has prevented you from building solid relationships if your network does not include mentors, advocates, and sponsors you can readily connect with.

When Autumn found herself in a cycle of dread for the next workday, she reached out to key mentors and advocates in her network for coaching to help navigate her thoughts and potential actions. Through those conversations, she gained the support to pursue a new role.

5. Do I know how to thrive and excel in my organization?

Understanding how to thrive and excel in any organization is critical to navigating your career. Your knowledge of cultural norms, both spoken and unspoken, critical skill sets, leadership attributes, and insights on how performance is evaluated in the organization will equip you to develop opportunities aligned with your career aspirations.

Autumn had clarity on how to thrive and excel in her organization. She understood the leadership attributes the organization valued and influential ways to broaden her scope and exposure through initiatives that aided her growth.

6. **Do I see opportunities to continue to excel in my organization, and are they aligned with my career interests?**

In the third question, you uncovered where your talents and passions aligned. Now consider where the opportunities are to excel in the specific role(s) aligned to your career interests. What are the existing avenues to pursue your career interests within your organization?

Are there roles readily available in which you have transferable skills? Reflect on developmental opportunities that would aid in growing your skills and help demonstrate your readiness for a new position. Additionally, consider how your leadership team or company supports you in exploring your career interests.

Although Autumn's current role was in a division that provided unique exposure and learning opportunities, she realized other paths within her organization would help her continue to pursue her aspiration to excel in an executive-level role. Autumn continued to feel invested in pursuing her aspirations.

7. Does my work environment encourage sharing my thoughts and experiences?

For Autumn, her work environment was not psychologically safe. There needed to be higher trust in sharing alternative ideas and thoughts, and forums did not foster thinking outside the box or trying new approaches. She found herself guarded when wanting to share her ideas and views. Over time, Autumn realized the environment would impact her confidence in her ability to perform and deliver results.

8. Do I feel confident in my ability to navigate my organization?

A level of savviness is needed to navigate organizational culture and understand how decisions are made to deliver results. The confidence in your ability to navigate your organization is less about your strength to do so and more about understanding the extent to which you may need to flex your style to be able to execute with impact. Consider how comfortable you are in the areas you may need to flex your style.

Based on how decisions were made, Autumn understood relationship management was critical in her organization. She learned to build strong working relationships that placed trust in the expertise and contributions of others. Her understanding helped her flex her style and position herself as a subject matter expert who delivered high-impact results.

Autumn had worked in several divisions before her current role, where she was comfortable navigating the environment. However, observing how others were navigating within her current group left her uneasy and unwilling to flex to mirror their approach.

9. Does my compensation allow me to live a lifestyle that aligns with my interests and responsibilities?

You should feel empowered to desire (and seek out) the compensation that will allow you to meet your needs—to live a lifestyle that aligns with your interests and covers your responsibilities.

You should feel valued for your contributions to the organization and be able to clearly differentiate yourself from others to command that value. To gain perspective on your value, revisit your performance evaluations and one-on-one conversations you reviewed in question two.

Autumn's lifestyle as a single woman with no children shifted to caretaker throughout her professional career. With expanded responsibilities to care for and support her family while pursuing interests in travel and art, she continues to re-evaluate her compensation on an annual basis as part of her ongoing tenacity to assess whether she's growing and well-placed in her organization.

10. Does my work and critical areas of my life (health, family, and personal relationships) integrate in an ideal way?

Sit with this question. Consider how each dimension of your life integrates (or doesn't). It's worth defining the ideal state in each of these areas. Balance may or may not be your objective.

For Autumn, her work triggered anxiety. Once she closed her laptop for the day, she had little desire for connection with family and friends. It took her more and more time to recharge for the next day. She had time for other areas, but the work environment drained her energy and desire.

All ten questions will help you assess key dimensions at the micro level and serve as inputs to consider at the macro level. At the micro level, several areas could have been better for Autumn. Assessing her current state helped Autumn determine that she needed to pursue a new opportunity.

She felt confident in finding a new role that would be more engaging and aligned with her career aspirations within her organization. However, she was prepared to consider external opportunities if the ideal position was unavailable.

Start assessing where you are as you think about what may be next for you. Use your responses to the self-assessment as a guide.

ASSESS WHERE YOU ARE
SELF-ASSESSMENT

To help you gain clarity and direction, complete the self-assessment on the following pages to assess where you are. Rate each area of your career on a scale of 1-5 (strongly disagree—strongly agree).

Rating Scale

1-Strongly Disagree

2-Disagree

3-Neutral

4-Agree

5-Strongly Agree

1. My current work is engaging and meaningful.

1-Strongly Disagree

2-Disagree

3-Neutral

4-Agree

5-Strongly Agree

2. My performance yields strong outcomes and impact on the organization.

1-Strongly Disagree

2-Disagree

3-Neutral

4-Agree

5-Strongly Agree

3. My talents and passions are aligned.

1-Strongly Disagree

2-Disagree

3-Neutral

4-Agree

5-Strongly Agree

4. I have a network of strong relationships that includes mentors, advocates, and sponsors.

1-Strongly Disagree

2-Disagree

3-Neutral

4-Agree

5-Strongly Agree

5. I have clarity on how to thrive and excel in my organization.

1-Strongly Disagree

2-Disagree

3-Neutral

4-Agree

5-Strongly Agree

6. I see opportunities to continue to excel in my organization aligned with my career interests.

1-Strongly Disagree

2-Disagree

3-Neutral

4-Agree

5-Strongly Agree

7. My work environment encourages me to share my thoughts and experiences.

1-Strongly Disagree

2-Disagree

3-Neutral

4-Agree

5-Strongly Agree

8. I feel confident in my ability to navigate my organization.

1-Strongly Disagree

2-Disagree

3-Neutral

4-Agree

5-Strongly Agree

9. My compensation allows me to live a lifestyle that aligns with my interests and responsibilities.

1-Strongly Disagree

2-Disagree

3-Neutral

4-Agree

5-Strongly Agree

10. My work and key areas of my life (health, family, and personal relationships) integrate in a way that is ideal for me.

1-Strongly Disagree

2-Disagree

3-Neutral

4-Agree

5-Strongly Agree

ASSESSMENT REFLECTION

Reflect on the areas you rated two and below (disagree and strongly disagree).

1. How are these areas impacting you?

2. How important are these areas to you?

3. What prevents these areas from being satisfied?

4. What would it take to shift these areas to your satisfaction?

STEP 2

DETERMINE WHAT YOU WANT

Meet Lena Brown
Age: 41
Industry: Financial Services
Marital Status: Married, two children

"What are you willing to do right now?" is the question Lena Brown sat with while bonding with her first child during maternity leave. She was ready to make a career pivot yet found herself contemplating what she wanted.

After receiving her MBA, Lena became interested in working with professionals across various roles and industries. Although she excelled in finance, she fell into the industry after shifting her pursuit from law school.

Following six months of potential career path discussions with her leader, it was clear Lena's leader (and the organization) wanted her to remain in finance. She felt undervalued and unheard in her desire to translate her finance skills and MBA experience into more strategic consultative opportunities.

Across the division, there were individuals pivoting from the traditional finance path. In Lena's observation, White men were primarily provided pathways to transition out of finance. While Lena was unaware of their available resources or the depth of their network, she lacked support to pursue alternate opportunities.

Lena had a choice to make.

She chose to return from maternity leave to the pharmaceutical company that paid for her MBA. Lena took what she thought would be a more strategic role in finance. Given the volume of organizational changes happening in the group, the role ultimately did not have the level of strategy she desired. After a year and a half of little headway, she determined it was time to leave.

In assessing where she was, Lena realized loyalty to her company kept her in a role that lacked alignment with her career interests. Because the organization paid for her MBA, Lena wanted to allow the company time to support her career aspirations. At the time, Lena's daughter was less than a year old when she determined it was time to leave. She wanted to do work she enjoyed, feel valued, and be fulfilled by her impact while navigating a new level of work-life balance. Lena's list of wants led her to outline the criteria for considering new opportunities. She prioritized challenging, meaningful work in the pharmaceutical industry that would afford her a work-life balance alongside a level of compensation that rewarded the expertise she would bring to a new organization.

As opportunities came about on LinkedIn, she expanded her industry considerations beyond pharmaceuticals. Lena explored options, including moving across the country to join a technology company or staying local to join a financial services organization. As she researched viable companies, she returned to the question, "What am I willing to do right now?"

WHAT'S YOUR ENDGAME?

When someone frustrated by their current role or work environment reaches out for coaching, I ask, "What's your endgame?"

I hear a spectrum of responses from I want "X" role to I want to negotiate my salary. Rarely does anyone lead with or connect their interest to pursue a new position to their endgame.

For Lena, her endgame of transitioning out of finance was ten years in the making. The clarity in her goal helped her focus on the skills and experiences she would gain and the business outcomes she would impact as she explored various roles, opportunities, and industries. It also allowed her to consider the risks and trade-offs she would be willing to make to pursue her endgame.

How does this decision (choosing a new role, moving for an opportunity, or increasing your salary) connect to your endgame?

Your endgame can serve as a guide. It will help you avoid hastily pivoting to the next role or company without alignment that continues to aid you in pursuing your ultimate goal. You should ensure if you're frustrated in your role or with your company, the next opportunity addresses that underlying frustration and supports you in achieving your endgame or career aspirations.

Consider what is most important to determine what you want across the assessed areas. Map out the potential ways you could address those areas. This analysis may require you to take exploratory actions specific to a field or interest.

Suppose your endgame is to create multiple streams of income to build generational wealth. In that case, there's a different level of importance on "my compensation allows me to live a lifestyle that aligns with my interests and responsibilities." And there is a greater emphasis on "my work along with key areas of my life (health, family, and personal relationships) integrate in an ideal way."

That importance may lead you to set salary targets that define the types of career opportunities you give a second look. Or it may lead you to explore how to reshape your career to incorporate other wealth-building ventures.

Once you've narrowed in on a few options, outline the worse-case scenario. Write out the scenarios to delineate from any story you may be telling yourself about potential opportunities and the perceived risk associated with choosing any of the options. It's important to discern if what you've categorized as risk is linked to your comfort level with risk. Free yourself from the belief that staying is always less risky than making a transition.

Lena weighed each of her new career options. She considered the company's success, her ability to move out of finance, the location, and the support (or lack thereof) she and her husband would have in various regions of the country. Lena determined moving across the country before her daughter's first birthday with little to no family support wasn't a trade-off she was willing to make. Lena prioritized staying local, with family near by, to join a company that would support her aspirations to move out of finance.

Meet Doc Wilson

Age: 37

Industry: Independent Investment Consultant

Marital Status: Single, one child

"I haven't defined a career yet, I'm just doing what I love to do and it happens to be benefiting myself and others," reflected Doc Wilson.

Doc is an independent consultant with 15 years of experience across the financial services and insurance risk management industries. Throughout his career, he has made several career transitions. Doc's primary considerations for determining whether to pursue a new opportunity have been monotonous work, stagnation, and the ability to continue to earn more.

His first career transition came after spending almost five years with a financial services firm. At the time, his fondness for the company outweighed his desire to increase his salary—he needed and deserved more to support his personal finance goals. Doc's financial goals led him to an investment role with a more significant sales-based compensation structure. He then pivoted from financial services to insurance, then transitioned to insurance risk management.

During the COVID-19 pandemic, Doc worked virtually for an insurance risk management company. As forwarded work calls and emails constantly buzzed on his cell, Doc felt an invasion of his privacy. He reflected, "There were too many people in my home, and I didn't like it."

He warned his job that better systems were needed to support the volume of business he had brought in on a new contract, yet he had no support. To cope with it all, Doc found himself napping between calls. Yes, napping! He literally took 10-minute naps between calls to distance himself from work.

"I'm at work, but my job doesn't know I quit," Doc laughed.

He was disengaged. Doc had quietly quit or rather dialed back by delivering the bare minimum. He hated his job and didn't want to work for someone else in the same environment he slept in. A change was sorely needed.

Doc knew he needed to find a role he would be passionate about—one where he could motivate and care for others while challenging the status quo within financial services. His desire led him to shift to an entrepreneurial path as an independent consultant. The autonomy to choose the clients he wanted to work with was part of the freedom that led and has kept him on the entrepreneurial path.

Now, Doc happily works for himself from the comfort of his home with a level of engagement and discipline throughout the day that doesn't lend to naps between calls. Grounded by his faith and through self-reflection, Doc explored various ways to best provide for his family. Ultimately, he wanted the ability to identify his client base, shift away from selling products directly to clients, and launch systems that could build his legacy. Doc rejects the notion that there is a lower risk of staying with an organization with high familiarity and comfort in the environment. His perspective has shifted how he weighs perceived risk in considering new opportunities.

Like Doc, you may determine your endgame has as much to do with achieving your financial goals as it does with avoiding monotonous work. Whatever your endgame is, your reflection will foster the clarity needed to determine what you want and help you consider your options beyond one dimension or factor.

How can you get closer to your endgame?

Step 3, strategizing your next best move, will provide insight on getting closer to your endgame.

STEP 3

STRATEGIZE YOUR NEXT BEST MOVE

Meet Kendall Reynolds
Age: 39
Industry: Construction Materials
Marital Status: Married, no children

"Your vision doesn't have to be completely teased out. Have your vision outlined. Then start to write down the important things that will help you get there," Kendall Reynolds highlighted.

Leading up to Kendall Reynolds's tenth year with a public accounting firm, she strategized an exit. Her blood pressure was getting out of control. She worked long hours and ate at her desk, only to realize she was almost killing herself. When Kendall's doctor asked her if she enjoyed being there, she decided it wasn't worth it. With the spark to exit, she began to explore new opportunities.

Familiarity kept Kendall at the public accounting firm for two additional years while she vetted what would be the ideal position and fit. Through the power of her network, a previous client presented an opportunity to transition from public accounting to an accounting role at a concrete and cement company. Kendall strategized how joining a smaller company could help her continue to excel. She thought about the new skills she would gain to equip her for a future transition to work for herself. Kendall outlined the benefits and created short- and long-term plans.

In the short term, the career transition afforded her exposure to a new industry, future roles on the financial side, and a great leader who affirmed her value. Kendall would have more time to explore her passion—curating experiences that create social connections. Long term, she could map out her ideas to transition into event planning with a timeline to secure her event space.

Although the transparency of how to climb the accounting ladder kept Kendall in a profession in which she's highly skilled, it misaligned with her passion and personality. She strategized the benefits within her current career that would fuel and prepare her to pursue her passion.

Your next best move should be the move that helps you make progress towards what you determine you want for your career—your endgame. It is not finite. You might take many paths and steps to strive towards your goal. Strategizing your next best move is about uncovering the options available and then narrowing down what is most appropriate to do next.

To effectively strategize your next best move, list several options you could take that align with your desires. Outline the benefits, drawbacks, and risks associated with each option. Define your worst-case scenario or least favorable choice and consider the likelihood and impact of each option. Reduce or mitigate any risk factors you have control over. Evaluate the timing based on your current circumstance and needs. Remove the adjective "perfect" from your evaluation to prevent you from staying longer than you should.

Depending on how you frame your criteria or considerations, a perfect time may not exist. Waiting until you receive that next bonus, or you've adjusted to being a working parent only places you in the next cycle of [insert thing]. You'll wait for that "thing" to happen to label the timing "perfect," and then there will be another life moment. Strategize the next best move for you, given where you are now and what you want.

To delineate, you might plan to wait six months to accomplish another goal or milestone, such as completing a training course that will set you up for success. That is an intentional, active decision. At all costs, avoid making the passive decision to wait until the perfect opportunity presents itself.

You have the power to identify the strides you might take towards any goal you aspire for yourself. If you are waiting for an opportunity you anticipate or have knowledge that will be available in the future, what are you doing in the meantime?

How are you preparing yourself if your next best move is to pursue a certification or degree within a specific timeline?

If your endgame is to launch a business that will run alongside your profession, how are you planning to manage both?

Creating a strategy that includes short-term and long-term plans will help center and prepare you to take a step.

Kendall asked herself all the hard questions to identify if the opportunity presented was a good fit. She prioritized her focus to see if she would receive what she needed personally and wanted out of a job.

For Kendall, transitioning to a smaller company had the benefit of lowering her stress, providing exposure to a new industry, and gaining a supportive leader who knew her work and would be an advocate. She could also expand her skills and learn valuable insights for her entrepreneurship endeavors.

Whether your career transition is entrepreneurship or another position within your company, it's essential to consider how this role, opportunity, or experience fits with what you want and the level of support or resources you will need to succeed during the transition.

MEET CONRAD HENDERSON

Age: 35
Industry: Retail Systems
Marital Status: Single, one child

"I wish I would've known to negotiate a larger raise and some form of commission for the business I was securing for the organization," stated Conrad Henderson.

Conrad Henderson had been hustling to fix his colleague's service mistakes. He traveled domestically and internationally with the sales team when he strategized his next best move within his software service company. Conrad helped the team meet the grand service delivery metrics guaranteed in the client sales pitches. Plus, he was uncovering new business.

Despite a title change with an expanded higher-level role, Conrad received no salary increase. It never dawned on him to negotiate a raise to include commission incentives. In two years, he generated $10 million in sales through problem resolution and solution designs that propelled the sales team to the Presidential Club while making under $70K.

Conrad's job gave him the adventure and

meaningful work he wanted, yet it lacked alignment with his desired compensation. He explored potential opportunities to increase his salary and support in continuing to excel in management. Conrad determined project management would be his next best move. He pursued internal roles with no success. Then an external door opened via his network.

Conrad agreed to a breakfast "meet and greet" to learn more. During the conversation, he was able to convey his value and impact. His breakfast introduction turned interview led to an offer for a project manager role with a $15K salary increase, plus quarterly bonuses for sales generation.

Before accepting the role, he met with his manager to share the offer. Conrad was willing to stay if there might be a similar internal opportunity. His manager was unable to counter the offer. Conrad didn't know what else to do but knew what he wanted. Conrad reviewed the offer and examined the benefits of the new role. He weighed out how much longer he perceived it would take for him to excel if he stayed. He valued the relationship with his current manager, but he knew he had to go to welcome the next thing. Conrad decided his next best move was to accept the offer.

Kendall and Conrad leveraged their network to help them learn more about potential opportunities. Conrad was willing to stay if his employer matched his external offer. Anchored by what he wanted, Conrad ensured he commanded the value he brought to an organization.

Both Kendall and Conrad understood how the role they considered could position them for their next opportunity. They found resolve in the benefits and trade-offs of potential moves they could make. Each was able to size up the risk involved. Strategizing their next best move helped them create a plan that prepared them to take a step.

STEP 4

TAKE A STEP

Meet Arthur Sholar

Age: 38
Industry: Electric Vehicles
Marital Status: Married, two children

"I was able to move pass my fear by realizing that if for some reason it didn't work out, I could go back to what I was doing, with comfort the opportunity would do wonders for my family," highlighted Arthur Sholar.

Arthur never envisioned that after 17 years of corporate experience working in the Southern region of the United States, he would relocate with his wife and children to his Midwest hometown for his dream job. Taking several steps over the latter six years of his career prepared him for an industry, career, and geographical transition.

Arthur began his career in the financial services industry. He spent nearly 11 years with his first firm focused on navigating how the organization expected him to show up. He adjusted his style, found ways to be disarming, and won others over.

At a critical point on a sales career path, he opted to take a step to pursue his interests in HR by accepting a role a level below. Seeing it as his best option to pivot to a new career path, he weighed his choices, negotiated to keep his salary, and took the step.

That step back in job level was a catalyst to build upon transferable skills. It helped him define and gain clarity on what he wanted. Following his transition to HR and with a growing family, he was ready to pursue external opportunities. Arthur then transitioned to another financial services company, where he worked for three years before the option to change industries and relocate presented itself.

A former colleague reached out to see if

Arthur would be interested in relocating to his hometown to join a start-up electric vehicle company. He was curious to learn more. The opportunity to join a hyper-growth company with the power to influence the organizational culture in his way while working for an organization with a greater purpose was an attractive offer.

Moving back home to the Midwest area was the next puzzle piece he needed. With the support of his family, Arthur took the step to move his family into his parent's basement apartment for nine months to ensure it was the right decision. *Sidebar-I'm not the only one strategizing basement apartments and parental living options*.

Arthur knew the trade-offs and the risk he was accepting with a move to join a start-up. He rationalized that he could return to his previous industry if it didn't work out. He positioned himself and his family to make a pivot if necessary.

Taking a step wasn't hard for Arthur because his children motivated him to overcome his fear.

Taking action allowed him to pursue a different path to provide more for his family and blossom into the person he was striving to become. Each career transition grew his confidence and preparedness for the next opportunity.

Being valued for his emotional intelligence, leadership skills, and business outcomes has afforded him the confidence to show up as his authentic self at work.

Gone are the days of fitting the mold of the organizational culture. Currently, Arthur fosters the organization's culture as Head of Belonging, rocking Air Jordan's on an accelerated path to equip him to become a Chief Diversity Officer. Arthur's ability to take steps has inspired his oldest child to pursue studies in science, technology, engineering, and mathematics.

It has also provided his wife the flexibility to pursue new endeavors in alignment with her passion. Not being paralyzed by fear allowed him to take a step.

MEET ROD JOHNSON

Age: 33
Industry: Investment Consultant
Marital Status: Divorced, three children

"You won't know if the value you bring matches the salary you should command until you put yourself out there to see or seek to command the value within your current organization," said Rod Johnson.

As an investment consultant, Rod spent ten years with one organization before moving to his current company. In the time leading up to his transition, he was content. However, Rod knew he wasn't where he wanted to be. When an external recruiter circled back regarding an opportunity, Rod declined a year prior, he knew company loyalty was the only thing holding him back. Rod was not being thought of for the internal roles which he had expressed an interest in.

Rod realized different aspects of the company culture had eaten away at him. He felt the pressure of perfection throughout his career, with a lot of value placed on building a network. He adjusted and saw the payoff, but it wasn't him. It took Rod six years into his tenure with the organization to shift his mindset to be himself, work hard, and be visible in more natural ways to him.

He wanted to feel valued for his contributions in monetary and non-monetary ways. Rod intentionally prepared for a promotion within his organization but was unsure if he had internal support.

He strategized his next best move thinking about the offer he received. The role would require a future move across state lines amidst marital separation. Rod shared the offer with his leader to fully explore if there was an opportunity to stay with the company and at least increase his salary in the interim of pursuing a promotion. Initially, the company expressed they couldn't match the offer, so he resigned with a month's notice. Shortly before his last day, the company countered with a salary increase slightly below the external offer to remain in his current role. At that point, it wasn't what he wanted.

Rod believed a salary increase and a new position would prove the company valued him. He had done the work of narrowing in on a path and networked along the way, yet the organization hadn't even thought of him when the role he was interested in became available.

Meanwhile an external organization intentionally pursued him—they wanted to build a relationship and foster a culture where Rod saw his value and ability to be himself comfortably.

For Arthur, an internal step to accept a lower role was the catalyst to pursue a different path. Then, taking action to relocate and change industries was another avenue to accelerate his growth within HR. It provided him with experience across several functions and helped him solidify his desire to become a Chief Diversity Officer.

Fear, apprehension, and doubt can prevent you from taking a step. The desire to take the perfect step or pursue a transition at the perfect time may keep you stuck. Rod and Arthur had courage, faith, and the willingness to bet on themselves. They were confident in their ability to thrive in a new opportunity or pivot if needed.

You can take a step while being scared. If you've done the work, you are not making a spontaneous or reactionary decision. You've assessed your desire and thought through your options and the impact of any path you might pursue.

There's learning and growth in every step you may take, but it begins with taking a step. Step 5 will guide you on how to maximize learning along your career transition journey.

STEP 5

REFLECT AND REDIRECT

Meet Gabriel Sydney

Age: 45
Industry: Financial Services
Marital Status: Married, two children

"I'm chasing happy. I don't want to sacrifice my mental health and work-life integration to move up; it's not worth it at this point," Gabriel Sydney smiled.

Following a transition from an eight-year career in the United States Air Force, Gabriel started an entry-level role at a financial services company. She excelled in a senior-level position in HR for 17 years, having held nine distinctly different roles with the organization.

Gabriel aspired to excel to an Executive HR role for her region. However, over time, the role no longer existed at the level she envisioned—yet that didn't stop her. She took on regional responsibilities alongside her current position. Gabriel's aspiration to excel while remaining within the regional office has come with its limitations. There have been fewer opportunities at higher levels and less exposure, resulting in Gabriel developing a strategy to navigate the limited opportunities available.

Until most recently, Gabriel has been committed to staying with her organization until early retirement. Three years into her current role, she reached the peak of her development, leading her to pursue internal and external opportunities to provide new growth and learning.

Gabriel's exploration has yet to yield a new role. A lot of self-reflection led Gabriel to redirect her aspirations to launch an HR consulting firm to expand her options. Although she never saw herself as an entrepreneur, Gabriel reshaped her thoughts on how she might achieve her endgame of early retirement while continuing to stretch herself. She is now redirecting to determine what strides she will make to best position her for later.

Gabriel awaits the next opportunity that aligns with her career interests and provides additional growth and development with a newfound openness to external possibilities through her consulting business. She is expanding her skill set and completing certifications to maximize her learning in her current role.

Gabriel is being strategic about the next move. She has prioritized her mental health and personal preferences to align with her next move. She is reflecting on the trade-offs and adjustments to her five-year timeline that may better position her to achieve her goals.

You will not have complete control over the outcome of your steps. If you aren't selected for the role or the program you've applied for, take some time to reflect. Reflect on the actions you've taken and where you've made progress. Consider what you've learned about yourself through new insights, then redirect as needed.

Each step may not yield periods of linear progression. However, upon reflection, it may be necessary to revisit previous steps to redirect your plan of action. Throughout Gabriel's career, she took linear steps that allowed her to advance. She had yet to experience feelings of stagnation. After reflecting on the outcome of several internal interviews, she redirected to broaden her external network and endeavors.

MEET LENNOX JEFFERSON

Age: 41
Industry: Financial Services
Marital Status: Divorced, one child

"Have discipline about ensuring your life is in alignment with the path you want to be on," stated Lennox Jefferson.

Lennox Jefferson sits down every quarter to ask herself if it's time to *stay or go.* First, she reviews her vision board and then her 15-year plan to assess where she sees herself and the current alignment. Lennox considers what certifications and other milestones will help position her to achieve her goals at the 15-year, five-year, one-year, and six-month markers.

Throughout her 20-year professional career, Lennox has made several career transitions. Some of those pivots were triggered by experiences from her team and company that did not foster a desire to stay. Even when Lennox is fulfilled, she checks in with herself to consider if her steps align with her aspirations to excel to the C-suite. For Lennox, her career has been built on a wide range of interests she explored through various career transitions that energized her.

Lennox launched a consulting firm intending to work for herself for one to two years to create time to complete additional certifications. Her consulting firm came about after an organizational exit in which she desired more flexibility in her life.

As Lennox's business grew, she redirected her intention by scaling her business, completing an Executive MBA, and pursuing an industry pivot post-graduation. Years later, when she was recommended for a new role with a key strategic initiative that would give her broader exposure, her excitement led her to take the role without being diligent in her alignment check of connection to her greater purpose.

Lennox immediately reaped the consequences and became disengaged from the team and work. Her day to day began to affect her health, mentality, and interactions with her parents, partner, and child.

She experienced anxiety—finding herself in extra therapy sessions to do the reflection work necessary to create a plan to redirect. The Assess Where You Are Self-Assessment helped Lennox identify the key area of impact—her current role was no longer serving her well. She shifted to leverage her network to determine if she should stay in the role, leave the organization, or seek a new position or path.

Lennox's "reflect and redirect" steps led her to revisit outlining what she wanted. She created a new set of "next best move" options. Ultimately, Lennox landed on maximizing her learning in the role for another six months until the ideal opportunity materialized. She then utilized her network within her organization to make a relatively quick pivot.

Lennox took a step that didn't serve her well, yet she recovered by reflecting and redirecting her efforts to strategize her next best move. Again, The Five Breakthrough Steps for Career Transitions™ are not always linear. You may find yourself revisiting previous steps, especially after you reflect and redirect.

PART III

PUTTING IT ALL TOGETHER

The previous chapters highlight how each step applied to a stage of career transition consideration. The following section pulls all the steps together to demonstrate how the Five Breakthrough Steps for Career Transitions™ unfold over the course of a person's career journey.

MEET VICTOR BULLSEYE

Age: 41
Industry: Technology
Marital Status: Married, three children

"I'm okay taking a risk on an opportunity that may not be greener because I'm confident in my abilities and okay with knowing I may not be at that organization in 10 years," Victor Bullseye said.

This mindset shift primed Victor to navigate leaving a financial services organization after a 12-year career across six roles. When Victor's third child was on the way, he realized he had been stalling on pursuing external opportunities out of comfort and stability in growing his career with one organization. His expanding family was a key motivator to seek new perspectives and broaden his experience. Victor wanted to see what else the world had to offer and test his ability to succeed elsewhere.

At the beginning of his career, Victor had no aspirations to work in Corporate America. The stories his parents shared over the dinner table with him and his sister about their experiences navigating Corporate America as Black professionals left him with no interest. Despite those dinner table conversations, he accepted an entry-level role at a financial services company intending to stay for a few years. Before he could plan his exit, a mentor offered him a unique opportunity to transition into Diversity and Inclusion (D&I). The offer from his mentor became a pivotal step to building a 15+ year career focused on advancing D&I initiatives in Corporate America.

Building a career in D&I has afforded Victor a lens into the journey organizations are on to foster inclusive environments, the impediments of organizational politics, and the value of great leadership. He has found his passion and purpose for being here on earth within his D&I career. He strives to become a change agent, impact people, and develop more productive, cohesive teams that drive company engagement. Victor wants to shift the dinner table stories of underrepresented groups. Ultimately, his endgame is to launch a Diversity, Equity, and Inclusion consulting firm.

Feeling stagnant in his ability to remain a change agent at the firm where he built his career, Victor knew it was time to strategize his next best move. He narrowed in on three key criteria for his next role— level of autonomy, decision-making, and demonstrated company commitment to advance D&I initiatives.

As he began to explore external opportunities, colleagues encouraged him to remain open to internal roles. Victor seemingly found himself as a final-round candidate for two distinctly different positions—one internal and one external. When it appeared he would not be selected for the external opportunity, he took the internal role. The internal role supported key initiatives that aligned with his passions and provided an opportunity to lead a team.

Victor continued to maintain the external relationships he had built. Shortly after the birth of his third child, the organization where he was a final candidate reached back out to offer him a role to create a new diversity recruiting strategy. Victor reflected on his choice to take the internal role several months later. He realized yet again it was comfort keeping him at the organization.

Victor knew it was time to leave, or he would question, in another 12 years, why he had not taken a risk or been confident in his abilities. Anchored by his passion and purpose, he ran towards the opportunity to build something new with a company within the insurance industry.

After three years with the insurance company, Victor became fatigued by the organization's lack of commitment, the pace of decision-making, and the number of teams that sought to provide input with no leadership accountability. He took a step to resign from the insurance company. When his leadership team countered his resignation by expanding his role with the promise to provide more support, he decided to stay.

Eight months later, a previous colleague, now working for a technology firm, reached out about an opportunity she thought would be a great fit. After meeting a dozen people, the technology company created a Global Diversity, Equity, and Inclusion Lead role for Victor.

Here he was, with yet another opportunity to build something new. He did his due diligence by assessing the company's mission and development opportunities. He weighed the pros and cons of transitioning from a large insurance company to a smaller tech firm. He prayed, mediated, and wrote out the decision impacts to ensure he was at peace in his heart and mind.

As Victor gained new mentors with more objective voices, his confidence in his ability grew, as did his comfort with the risk of pursuing another transition. Even if the next organization wasn't a good fit, Victor affirmed his decision and ability to make the career transition. He wished he had more people encouraging him earlier in his career and life—reminding him that he and his family would be okay, he's smart, and he will figure out how to thrive.

Victor's ability to navigate several career transitions internally and externally is a testament to The Five Breakthrough Steps for Career Transitions™. In each career transition, he determined what was most important to him in the next opportunity, considered the impacts of pursuing various options, and took a step. Over time, Victor reflected and redirected when his current position no longer served him well.

It took Victor years to feel comfortable leaving an organization. His career transitions have become easier since the first one because he knows what to expect.

He knows what's most important to him. He is anchored in his passion and purpose, guided by his desire to make a lasting impact for future generations, and progressing toward his endgame.

MEET KAM EMMANUEL

Age: 46
Industry: Business Consulting and Coaching
Marital Status: Married, two children

"What's your 'why'? I had the title, I crossed the six-figure mark, but I was deflated," said Kam Emmanuel.

After university studies, Kam became a teacher working with young students in foster care who were excluded from the school system. Feeling she was unable to make a difference led her to pursue a career transition to become a United Kingdom diplomat. Kam's diplomacy career spanned 17 years before she took an early retirement package.

Eight years into her second career, Kam contemplated whether she should continue serving as HR Director for a municipality or whether it was time to go again.

The second phase of Kam's career led her to move to the southern area of the United States. Despite her career as a United Kingdom diplomat, it was challenging for an organization to value the wealth of her experience. To get her foot in the door, Kam took a telemarketer role in the local municipal police department. She spent three months strategizing how she could transition into HR. Despite wowing the interview team for a mid-level position, Kam was not selected given she had less than six months tenure at the company.

The municipality opted to choose another internal candidate. When they followed up to ask if she would be open to the front desk HR administrative role reporting to the HR Director, Kam sat with this option for a couple of days.

Kam decided her next best move was to take the role. Her title was HR Front Desk Administrator, yet she chose to embody the mindset of a CEO. Kam sought out opportunities to improve the operations. She took on special projects and initiatives, genuinely taking to heart the other duties as assigned in her job description. Five months later, she transitioned to a mid-manager position, and in two years, she became the HR Director.

During a company retreat, personal reflection led her to realize that she would be a life coach if she weren't in her current career. Kam decided to complete a yearlong coaching program. She then found an internal opportunity to pitch a coaching offer for executives and employees retiring from the municipality. Kam thought about resigning to pursue coaching full-time, but she was hesitant. She was successful at her organization; she had mastered how to excel from HR Administrator to HR Director.

Kam questioned if her embodiment of a CEO mindset would translate to her attaining success as an actual CEO of her own coaching and consulting firm. Kam found herself questioning if she should stay or go every year. Finally, she took a step to leave out of pure burnout. For five months, she went to work for another municipality. When the opportunity presented itself to return as HR Director, she went back to her former municipality on her terms—commanding the treatment she wanted.

Meanwhile, she had clarity that empowering lives through coaching was what she truly desired to do. The more successful she became, the more she found herself distant from directly helping people. She spent more and more time on strategy and execution with fewer opportunities to coach others. The ember flickering inside to coach and empower others dwindled.

Kam began strategizing her next best move again. She embarked on a season of preparing and learning what it meant to become an entrepreneur. She gained business management insights and worked on her coaching craft by gaining certifications. Kam worked to ensure she set herself up to leave without the need to go to another company. She set her vision and efforts on leaning wholly into launching her business—Keep Evolving Consulting.

When delayed grief of personal losses and parking lot protests in her police district intersected, Kam hit her lowest mental point. She chose to prioritize self-care by taking five weeks off, and the answer became unequivocal—it was time to leave her job.

Kam resigned from her employer and gained them as her first consulting client. Sitting with her why, taking a season to prepare, and using her job to fuel her passion equipped her to leave. The transition didn't happen overnight. When the opportunity or environment was no longer serving Kam, she reflected and redirected. Each step of the way, she re-strategized her next best move to ensure she maintained alignment with what she wanted and then took steps to continue to progress.

NOW WHAT?

Your decision on whether to stay or go depends on assessing where you are and determining what you want. Those two steps create the anchors that guide you in strategizing your next best move.

Your career vision may be a sketch or a beautifully crafted mural. Either way, being grounded in your endgame will allow you to take a step to help you walk toward your vision. Only you can best outline your reasons and assess them. There's a risk in staying or going. You know what you seek to gain or sacrifice on either path.

Actively decide which step you want to take. You have the power to walk toward the life you want for yourself and your family. Despite the distance between where you are today and where you seek to be, it starts with taking a step.

Taking a step becomes easier when you've engaged in the work. If you haven't addressed your fear, or you're over-indexing on the risk without finding ways to build the comfort and confidence you need to pursue a transition, you may find yourself staying in a career or role much longer than you should.

Your commitment to reflect and redirect as needed will help you identify where to re-strategize or further refine your transition plan. If you aspire to more, want to continue to learn, grow, and live your life's legacy in every season, then my question is— *now what?*

If you've been stuck or overwhelmed by where to begin and feel daunted by the road ahead, I hope Five Breakthrough Steps for Career Transitions™ support your journey. I hope the career stories woven throughout assure you there are others with similar experiences and provide the fuel to energize you for the road ahead.

Gone are the days of choosing a profession you must stay in until retirement.

You can pursue career transitions. You can leave environments that are no longer serving you. You can command the value you deserve. You can explore your options. You can stay, you can go, and you can return. You are enough. You are deserving. You belong even if you see no one who looks like you. Continue to revisit whether to stay or go.

Where will you go from here?

AUTHOR'S NOTE

In 2021, I took a step to connect with my friend Jossalyn Wilson to learn more about her publishing company. I was ready to stop sitting on the idea I had to write this book. I was prepared to move past fear.

Some fears were rooted in how I might be perceived for writing a book on career transitions and the intentional choice to weave in the narratives of Black professionals. Other fears were rooted in imposter syndrome.

Who was I to think that I was credible enough to write a career transition book. My coaching passion had been manifesting into a focus on career transitions for quite some time. It was the realization in coaching conversations that a framework to help guide professionals, especially Black professionals, through considering any career transition decision was necessary.

Each narrative highlighted in the book is based on real career experiences with fictitious names included, except for Kam Emmanuel. Kam welcomed the opportunity to be highlighted as herself. Many of the professionals who shared have made subsequent career transitions since their interviews for this book. I am grateful to be amongst a network of Black professionals seeking to make an impact and live out their life's legacies. Thank you to everyone in my network who entrusted me with their career transition story. This book is uniquely made because of you.

Like several people highlighted in the text, the question of whether to stay or go has continued to resurface throughout my career. While writing this book, I continued to live my career transition story. The Five Breakthrough Steps for Career Transitions™ truly helped me discern several career opportunities. I am affirmed that no matter what future career transitions I pursue, "I am too smart, I will be okay, my family will be okay, and I will figure out how to thrive."

AUTHOR'S BIO

Rebecca Taylor has 15 years of Human Resources experience across Talent Management. She has nearly ten years of executive coaching experience supporting clients within the financial services, higher education, healthcare, and nonprofit sectors. Rebecca utilizes a change coaching process and embraces a solution-based approach to partner with her clients to help them create and execute a plan of action to address their goals or challenges. She is passionate about coaching clients through facilitated self-discovery to identify ways to be the best version of themselves.

Rebecca primarily coaches mid-to-senior level professionals along their leadership journey to support advancement to broader leadership roles and through career transitions. She holds an MBA with an Executive Coaching Certificate and coaching certification from the International Coaching Federation.

Follow Rebecca online:
Web: https://taylorexecutivecoaching.com

Instagram: @TaylorExecutiveCoaching

www.ingramcontent.com/pod-product-compliance
Lightning Source LLC
Chambersburg PA
CBHW051539120626
46551CB00013B/1292